From a young age, Tanaz Ghaffarsedeh has been deeply fascinated by music, art, and philosophy. Growing up in an academic family, she was fortunate to have a mother who nurtured her creative side with an open mind.

From early childhood, she felt a profound connection to the voice of the universe and her intuition, often questioning the purpose of existence. As the youngest in her family, she spent much of her time alone, which allowed her to develop a deep relationship with her inner voice and the language of the universe.

Knowing that traditional schooling was not the right path for her, she pursued music with her mother's support. She studied 20th century composition and opera in Glasgow and later earned a master's degree in composition in London.

Beyond music, Tanaz also works as a photographer and video producer. Her latest work, *Sun,* which came out as an EP, is an audio-visual work which takes us on a journey from the lower vibration to higher vibration. It is very tied to this book, but in the form of music and visuals.

As spirituality and the art of stillness have always been closest to her heart, she wrote this book to share her experiences, hoping to offer guidance and insight to humanity.

I dedicate this book to my parents, who are no longer on this earth. They were my guiding lights, teaching me by example how to live with honesty, selflessly, patiently, and kindness.

Tanaz Ghaffarsedeh

FEED THE SOUL NOT THE EGO

AUSTIN MACAULEY PUBLISHERS®
LONDON * CAMBRIDGE * NEW YORK * SHARJAH

Copyright © Tanaz Ghaffarsedeh 2025

The right of Tanaz Ghaffarsedeh to be identified as author of this work has been asserted by the author in accordance with sections 77 and 78 of the Copyright, Designs and Patents Act 1988.

All rights reserved. No part of this publication may be reproduced, stored in a retrieval system, or transmitted in any form or by any means, electronic, mechanical, photocopying, recording, or otherwise, without the prior permission of the publishers.

Any person who commits any unauthorised act in relation to this publication may be liable to criminal prosecution and civil claims for damages.

A CIP catalogue record for this title is available from the British Library.

ISBN 9781037101625 (Paperback)
ISBN 9781037101632 (ePub e-book)

www.austinmacauley.com

First Published 2025
Austin Macauley Publishers Ltd®
1 Canada Square
Canary Wharf
London
E14 5AA

I am grateful to my mother, whose open-mindedness allowed me to dream freely. She taught me to pursue my passions with courage and to never be confined by society's expectations.

Above all, I want to thank my guiding angels. I truly believe this book was not written by me alone but was inspired by a higher power. Before I began writing, I had a dream in which a golden angel handed me a book and urged me to begin. The next day, I opened my laptop, and the words flowed effortlessly, as if they were being channelled through me rather than created by my own mind.

For this reason, I take no credit for writing this book. I am simply a vessel, and I am profoundly grateful to the guiding angels for using me as a messenger to share this wisdom.

'There is a light at the end of the tunnel'. Is this really true?

Or the real truth is, 'There is already a light within the tunnel connected with your soul, and you will be able to see it only if you are truly awakened'.

'Everything will be ok'. Is this really true?

Or the real truth is, 'Everything is already ok'.

"Embrace your time on this earth within each moment, as each moment is your moment of peace and shine. Each moment is a lesson, and a chance to remember. Bringing us closer to our real self, which is our immortal soul."

We are living in a dream; let your dream be kind, loving, and inspiring. Attachment is an illusion, as we are just in one big dream.

We will keep coming back until we learn all our lessons, the lessons that teach us we are all one, to be kind, and loving, and to do everything from the heart and the soul.

We live in a society where what we hear and learn shapes our understanding of truth. Every few centuries, a courageous individual emerges, offering a new 'truth'. We call it a new religion, a new leader, or a new philosophy. Yet the deepest truth has always been within each of us—waiting to be uncovered if we only listen to our inner voice.

What is truth?

Are we wired to follow one another?

Are we born with an innate desire to seek truth from others?

Do we find comfort in discovering a set of beliefs or rules that we can call our own?

What does it mean to be an individual in this vast world?

Why, as humans, do we feel the need to label everything, as if naming something gives us a place to belong?

Aren't the real questions those truths already known to us, deep within our hearts and souls?

The real question is: why can't we simply be free?

There are no names, labels, rules, or boxes—just pure freedom. We live life guided by our hearts and souls, unbound and unmarked by external constraints.

This freedom is our true inheritance, the same freedom we experienced as children—before fear took root.

It is a freedom filled with pure love, untouched by the limitations we learn as we grow.

Why are we here, and why do we keep returning? What is our true purpose?

Whether we were born in this century, the last, or many centuries ago, our lives as humans have evolved in ways once unimaginable. Not long ago, holding a phone in our hands was merely a dream, a fantasy. Travelling from one land to another by air seemed like an impossible illusion. A simple cold or flu could mean death, and the light that now illuminates our homes was once only a figment of imagination. Indeed, we have evolved—each century birthing new ideas, ideas that were once nothing more than dreams.

Throughout human history, our focus on material growth has been impressive, but it has also come with consequences. While we've advanced in many ways, this progress often distracts us from deeper truths and connections. When we take a step back and view life from a broader perspective, we may realise that what truly matters goes beyond the material— things like our relationships, values, and the well-being of our planet.

Enlightenment and awakening are terms we often use to describe our connection with our true selves. At their core, they are simple concepts, but the names themselves can evoke strong reactions. Many people quickly associate these terms with spirituality or religion when they hear them, which often shapes their response before they fully comprehend the meaning.

Some might dismiss the idea outright, saying, "I'm not into spirituality or religion, so this isn't for me."

Others might express mild curiosity but excuse themselves with, "That sounds interesting, but I don't have time for such things." These responses often stem from preconceived notions and the natural tendency of the judgemental mind to categorise and dismiss unfamiliar ideas.

Interestingly, when we avoid labelling the concept and instead explain it in straightforward terms – focusing on the essence of reconnecting with one's true self – the reactions are often very different. Without the trigger of a name, the judgemental mind is less likely to leap to conclusions, and people engage more openly.

This shift happens because, in its natural state, the judgemental mind isn't inherently dismissive. It becomes reactive when faced with fear or unfamiliarity. By presenting ideas in a way that bypasses these triggers, we can foster genuine curiosity and deeper understanding, breaking through the barriers of assumption and resistance.

What is enlightenment, or what does it mean to be awakened? How would we describe it if we had to put it into words? Enlightenment is freedom—a liberation from the illusions and limitations we impose on ourselves. Awakening is the process of remembering who we truly are. It's a realisation that we are far more than the roles we play or the identities we adopt. We are free, we are powerful, and we are so much more than we often believe ourselves to be.

It's actually quite simple—it's a doorway to heaven, a path to peace and light. We all have access to it because we are all souls. Yet, many of us have forgotten this truth as we navigate life. We are here on earth to learn lessons, to remember who we truly are, and to reconnect with our soul—a soul unburdened by the emotional baggage we, as humans, have created for ourselves.

The sooner we recognise this and unite with our soul, the sooner we can experience heaven. This isn't a distant, otherworldly place; it's the state of pure light and harmony where our soul originates. Unfortunately, the human mind often creates emotions and attachments that lower our vibrations, casting shadows that create an illusory darkness.

Heaven and darkness coexist here on earth. Heaven is the pure light that resides within us, waiting to shine. By releasing the illusions of the mind and embracing our soul's essence, we can transform our experience and see the heaven that is already around us.

The only requirement is to trust and reconnect with your true self. From that place, you will begin to see, feel, and experience things beyond explanation—true miracles that are inherent to all of us as humans. This is the power gifted to us by God, the universe, or whatever name resonates with you.

It is a divine gift, and it is the essence of who we truly are—the real, authentic self.

It's never too late to reconnect with your true self, no matter where you are in life. Time is just an illusion—don't let it define you or hold you back. At any age, under any circumstance, the moment you find this connection, you will uncover your magic and blessings.

This journey doesn't follow the rules of logic, because logic belongs to the mind, while true knowing resides in the heart. Our soul speaks through the heart, while our human identity is rooted in the mind. By aligning with your heart, you can transcend the limits of time and logic, embracing the truth of who you really are.

With each body comes a unique personality, shaped by the ego. The ego forms as we navigate the world, but as we deepen our understanding and remember our true essence, a moment will come when the ego begins to fade away—a symbolic death of the ego. For some, this awakening happens early in life; for others, it may come much later. If we believe in reincarnation, perhaps older souls – those who have journeyed through many lifetimes – face these lessons sooner, guiding them to remember who they truly are. The death of the ego does not mean the loss of our human self. Instead, it is the emergence of profound peace and the feeling of arriving home—our soul's true home. When this happens, we become vessels of light, illuminating the path for others. We transform into lightworkers, guiding and inspiring others to find their way back to the light.

Have you ever witnessed someone nearing the end of their journey on this earth? It is an incredibly beautiful sight. In those final moments, you can see a radiant light surrounding them. Their face becomes serene, and a brilliant glow shines through their eyes. There's a smile that comes from within, a deep, unspoken happiness that emanates from their soul as if they've found peace and fulfilment. It's a powerful reminder of the profound beauty of life's transitions.

I remember one evening when we visited my grandmother. That night, it felt as though I was seeing a completely different person. When she opened the door, there was a radiant light around her face, and her eyes sparkled with a special glow. Her smile was unlike any other—a smile filled with genuine joy. Most of all, there was a peaceful energy about her that I had never noticed before.

I spent no more than half an hour in the kitchen, sorting through her fridge when suddenly I heard a sound—an incredibly loud noise, almost as if the entire house had come crashing down.

The sound came from her bedroom. My mother and I rushed to see what had happened, and there she was – unconscious on the floor, wearing her praying gown – but her face was glowing, radiant like a star. She had suffered a severe stroke while praying.

A few days later, while in a coma at the hospital, she passed away. Did she know it was her time? Why was she so peaceful in her final moments? And why did she radiate that light? These questions linger as if her soul was preparing for its journey with calm and grace.

I also remember one night when I was about to fall asleep next to my father while my mother was finishing her evening chores. That night, my father had a large, peaceful smile on his face—he truly looked content. I watched him as he drifted off to sleep, his face glowing with a serene light, his body completely relaxed. He was smiling even in his sleep. Just as I was about to fall asleep, I heard a sudden sound from him. I don't recall much after that, as I was only seven years old, but I do remember my mother coming into the room and quickly taking me next door. I never fully comprehended the events of that night, but my father passed away a week or two later. A sudden heart attack had claimed his life.

Did he know it was his time? Why was he so peaceful? Why did he radiate such light and joy that evening? These questions still linger, as if his soul had already found peace before his body left this world.

Another memory takes me back to my mother. She had cancer, but the doctors couldn't pinpoint its origin. By the time they diagnosed her, it had already spread throughout her entire stomach area. She was in stage four when they finally discovered it, and at that point, the chances of saving her were extremely low.

For nine months, my mother fought the illness with incredible strength. It was in the last two months that we witnessed her rapid deterioration. Her body grew weaker, and her face changed in a way I could hardly recognise. She no longer looked like herself. The suffering was visible in her expression, and we truly began to understand what suffering really means.

During those final months, my mother seemed different in more ways than one. She began speaking to and communicating with invisible beings—presences that I couldn't see, but she could. It was as though her connection to another realm was growing stronger, something beyond our understanding at the time.

A week or two before she passed, something remarkable happened—her body appeared healthier. Her face became lighter, and her smile returned, this time with a true sense of happiness and peace. She seemed to regain her essence, the peaceful self we had known before the illness took its toll. As her passing drew nearer, this transformation deepened each day.

On the day she left us, I saw her lying on the bed, her face glowing with a radiant light surrounding her. She wore a peaceful smile, a serene expression that seemed to come from within as if she had found the ultimate peace before moving on.

We've now witnessed three different individuals, each experiencing a similar peaceful transformation as they neared the end of their lives. This raises the question: What is the reason behind this shared experience? And how did each of them sense that it was their time to go?

What we can understand from these experiences is that everyone knew it was their time because their intuition guided them—meaning their soul became stronger than the ego and took over their entire being. In that moment, the soul transcended the emotional baggage of the ego, replacing it with peace and love. This is the language of the soul, the language of the universe, and the language of God.

It is in those moments that they let go of their ego and the attachments it brings. They lose their sense of personality and begin to unite with their soul—their true self. In this union, they find peace at last. As they connect with their soul, they are granted a deep, hidden knowledge—a knowing that transcends the material world.

This experience is not unlike what happens when we fall ill. Have you ever noticed that when someone is sick, they often become a kinder, gentler person? Or when someone loses a loved one, they seem to soften, becoming more peaceful. This is because, in the face of pain and loss, we begin to detach from earthly attachments. We seek meaning in these experiences, but we don't need to endure pain or loss to connect with our souls. There are other ways, such as simply quieting the mind. We don't need to wait until our time comes to 'go home' to unite with our soul. We can begin this process right now, while living on this earth, by simply stilling our minds and reconnecting with the essence of who we truly are.

Then some seem to carry a light, a sense of peace, and inner happiness with them while they're here on earth. They move through life radiating this light, and it must feel truly amazing. This is what it means to live close to your soul, to be enlightened while still on this earth. Everything is light, everything is energy, everything is vibration—everything is one, and everything is God.

In this book, you will encounter many questions about finding happiness from within—questions about purpose, love, and more. These are questions that only your true self can answer. The answers lie within you, not in external sources. When a child asks countless questions, it's because they are still closely connected to their soul. As adults, we often stop asking 'why', but 'why' is one of the most powerful questions we can ask. It holds the key to unlocking doors of true understanding and inner wisdom.

True peace is a gift we can give ourselves. We don't have to wait for illness, loss, or the end of life to experience it. We can choose to live each day with happiness and peace, embracing it in every moment.

A section of this book is devoted to exploring 'darkness', which represents the emotions linked to attachment. It's crucial to understand how to find happiness within this darkness. As we all know, life is not always an easy journey. We must sometimes experience darkness to discover light or at least understand darkness to choose the light.

This book features short stories that illustrate life's journey through various stages of darkness. It is often said that individuals with extensive experience find light surrounding them, as they've lived through the challenges of dark emotions. With each experience, they learn how these emotions affect their lives, and the next time darkness arises, they no longer become entangled in it. However, as we've discussed, we don't need to wait until we experience darkness—we can learn from others and use their stories as valuable examples to guide our own path.

Each soul comes into this world to bring joy and peace. Within us, we carry both heaven and earth. But what does heaven truly mean? What is the significance of earth? And what do light and dark represent? These are the questions that invite us to explore the deeper truths within ourselves and the world around us.

Heaven exists within us, known by many names such as God, the universe, or energy. Our souls are connected to the abundant gifts the universe offers. To receive these gifts, we must connect with our soul through the power of perseverance—a power that allows us to see and feel beyond the limits of possibility. It's a force that transcends what we think we deserve or what we believe we can achieve. It's the alignment with our soul, the union with our true home.

The earth is a school for the ego, where its primary focus is on the material world. The ego—also known by other names such as the mind—is deeply connected to this earthly realm, driven by endless desires. The more the ego acquires, the more it craves, leading to dissatisfaction and inner turmoil. This dissatisfaction fuels the suffering we experience—wars, disappointments, pain, manipulation, lies, cheating, depression, theft, conflicts, arguments, and so much more. These actions, rooted in the ego, are the sources of suffering in both the world and human nature.

In today's world, we are born into a life shaped by what we see around us. We become caught up in the pursuit of 'things', constantly striving to accomplish more. For example, have you ever heard the phrase, 'Lucky kids, they're so happy—they have no worries and are content with the simplest things'?

Children's deep connection to their souls explains this. They naturally do things that bring their souls joy, and they are not yet concerned with the material world because they have not yet developed an 'ego'. Without an ego, they are free—they are not confined by the mind. They see and feel the endless delights that surround them. Whatever they do, they pour their full energy into it, and that becomes nourishment for their soul. When they act with pure hope and enthusiasm, they are living in harmony with their true selves.

Life and our upbringing can gradually cause us to forget our true purpose. Over time, we rely on the ego as a survival mechanism, losing sight of the fact that our main mission is to reconnect with our true selves. When we do this, we can shine, but without it, we struggle, endlessly seeking temporary pleasures and distractions. We are here to fulfil our soul's mission—bringing light to this earth.

This is where gambling, drugs, alcohol, cheating, and stealing come into play—these are all acts of the ego, not the soul. The soul, being a part of God, is pure light. It does not seek to bring suffering to you or those around you. Its true desire is to bring you joy, a joy that requires no external source, but rather the gift that has already been given to you. This gift is life itself, and it exists within every single person. Some are fortunate enough to tap into it, while others have forgotten how to use it. However, we must not judge ourselves or others. Everything is part of a greater picture. Nothing is inherently right or wrong; it is all an illusion. If an action does not align with the soul, one can choose to replace it with something that brings joy to the soul. It is really that simple.

We can divide the ego into three parts: the parent, the adult, and the child. For example, an artist may predominantly develop their child ego, expressing creativity and spontaneity. A person in finance is more likely to develop their adult ego, focused on logic, structure, and decision-making. A nurse, on the other hand, may primarily embody the parental ego, centred around care, responsibility, and nurturing others.

Understanding our ego is essential to mastering our relationship with it, allowing us to control it when necessary. By becoming familiar with our own ego, we improve our ability to communicate with others, as we can better grasp the true meaning behind their words. This awareness makes it easier to set the ego aside and connect with our soul. It's like the saying, 'Keep your friends close and your enemies closer'. While we're not labelling the ego as an enemy, it can certainly feel like one if we don't know how to let go of it when it takes control.

The true purpose and accomplishment of our humanity are not rooted in the material world—things like jobs, money, status, or relationships. While these things are important for our experience on earth, it's not about accumulating them but about how we attain them and maintain them without losing connection to our souls. It's about learning how to be truly satisfied.

Please note that satisfaction, in this context, doesn't mean avoiding hard work. It means being at peace, fully embracing each moment, not dwelling on the past or worrying about the future and being grateful for what you have in the present. Live fully and pour your energy into the moment you're experiencing. Love life unconditionally, just as life loves you unconditionally.

We often try to control every moment of our lives, but what if we let go of that control and trust that a greater force is guiding us? Work hard, have courage, and be kind, but release the need to control, and watch as miracles unfold. This is what it means to have trust and faith in a higher power—recognising that this higher power is also within you, as your higher self.

Have the courage to pursue your goals but find contentment in the present moment. Don't dwell on yesterday or worry about tomorrow—be happy with now. You will find peace of mind and connect with your true self in the now. It will heal you. Focusing on the present is like a child fully immersed in the task at hand, pouring all their energy into the moment. When you focus on now, your soul can shine through you, free from the distractions of past regrets or future anxieties. Remember, there is no timeline—everything is unfolding in the present. So, embrace the moment and be truly present.

Have you ever had a dream at night that later came true? This happens because, when we sleep, our mind is at rest, allowing our soul to connect with us freely. Without the constraints of time, we can travel through different dimensions in our dreams and receive insights that can enhance our own lives and the lives of others.

Once you connect with your true self, you'll use that knowledge to enlighten and help others. This means discovering the area in which you can make an impact. For example, Bill Gates found his calling through his enlightenment, which gave him the courage to pursue a career dedicated to helping others. Similarly, Albert Einstein, through his insight, dared to share groundbreaking knowledge with humanity—wisdom that continues to be valued and relevant many years later.

Each of us is born with courage, kindness, talent, and a unique voice. The world is abundant with love, peace, and everything good, available for everyone to embrace. All we need to do is believe, listen, and look beyond what we already know. This is the essence of the law of attraction.

You must ask, believe, and hold onto hope. You must have courage and envision the desired outcome. Be patient, do good along the way, and in the end, you will receive what you seek.

If you can dream it, it means that in another timeline, it's already yours. This is why we have unique dreams and hopes—each of us is aligned with a different vision. If we can dream it, it's already on its way to us.

Being awakened means reconnecting with the entire universe and with God. We are all one, each carrying the spirit of God within us. All we need to do is listen and awaken to the boundless love that is always available to us.

Prayer is religious, and meditation is spiritual, yet both serve the same purpose: to quiet the mind (ego) and connect with your soul. The wisdom found in all religions and spiritual beliefs carries the same message: your true purpose on this earth is enlightenment. When you awaken, you tap into boundless love and courage to live fully.

We all carry a light within us; we just need to awaken to it. Darkness does not belong to the soul; it is merely a thought that the ego clings to. It is nothing but a pure illusion.

Light is the true home of your soul, while darkness is the realm of the ego. Both are forms of energy and vibration. Light carries a higher vibration, bringing clarity, peace, comfort, love, and true hope. In contrast, darkness holds a lower vibration, feeding the ego with fear, guilt, jealousy, lies, attachment, illusion, control, and many other energies. Interestingly, the list for the ego is much longer than that of the soul. The soul is pure light, simple and serene, while the ego thrives on complexity, which is why its list of influences is so much longer.

The question is: where are you, and where do you want to be? Do you choose simplicity or complexity? Do you opt for peace or chaos? Ultimately, it is a choice you make for your time here on earth, guided by your free will.

Do good, be kind, embody love, be pure, and act without condition. Unconditional love comes from the soul, which knows no limits or expectations. When you give unconditionally, you experience true freedom—free from attachment, expectation, or fear of not receiving. It is pure magic.

This concept also applies to games, as explored by Eric Berne in his book on the subject. Games can only exist when people communicate through their egos. The soul does not engage in games, as it is beyond such complexity.

True love and genuine kindness are unconditional, without barriers. When love stems from the ego, however, games begin to play out, and the experience becomes less pleasant—often turning hostile. The ego's need for validation forms the foundation of this conditional kind of love. In contrast, real, unconditional love is kind, compassionate, and eternal. It remains unshaken, rooted deeply within, no matter the circumstances.

It's important to understand that if you give love and kindness with the expectation of receiving something in return, it is not truly love. It is love rooted in the ego. Genuine love and kindness are characterised by their selfless nature, given freely and without any expectation.

Love takes many forms—from a mother's love for her child to the bond between siblings, partners, and beyond. Similarly, our souls embody love, kindness, and compassion. The soul is eternal, never dying, while it is only the ego that fades away. The essence of who we are, our soul, remains infinite and untouched by time.

Take the time to truly connect with your soul, for it is the source of your deepest happiness and joy. Your soul is the essence of who you are—the light and stars that reside within you. It is your unique radiance, so honour it, cherish it, and let it shine brightly. And when you encounter another soul, recognise their light and reflect the same respect and kindness.

We are all incredibly special, connected to one another and the universe, each a part of the divine.

This book is structured into chapters, each outlining a step in the journey toward enlightenment. With every chapter, you will be presented with real-life examples that you may find relatable to your own experiences. The book delves into the emotions that lead us into darkness and contrasts them with the essence of our true selves, which guides us toward the light—what we often refer to as heaven.

This is a healing book—one that has the potential to transform your life for the better. It explores the full spectrum of our emotions and behaviours, examining both the darkness and the light within us. Rather than telling you what to do, this book offers deep insights and explanations, leaving the choice of your path entirely up to you. It respects your free will, empowering you to decide where you want to go on your journey.

Throughout this book, you will find short stories that accompany each lesson. With each story, you will walk through the life of another, gaining new perspectives. The teachings in this book do not instruct you to follow the same path. Rather, they open your mind to the possibilities of awakening. You are the creator of your own life, and through the wisdom gained from this book, other sources, and your own experiences, you will have the tools to craft your version of heaven.

In this book, you will find a series of exercises designed to help you build a deeper relationship with yourself—both your ego and your soul. These exercises will also guide you toward a greater understanding of others, fostering compassion and connection.

Exercise 1

Before you read this book, have a pen and paper ready and write down your experiences through your life that were challenging, and then write down how you overcame them. What emotions did you experience? If there were any people involved, how did you deal with them?

The key to peace and enlightenment lies in how we respond to the challenges life presents us with. In every situation, you have a choice: you can choose anger, bitterness, depression, and hopelessness, or you can choose hope, trust, and peace, understanding that everything happens for a reason. These experiences are here to awaken you, heal you, and teach you valuable lessons. Life's circumstances will pass, but your higher self – the essence of who you truly are – will remain. Therefore, it is essential to prioritise your well-being and growth, embracing each moment as it comes.

Remember, no situation or another person is responsible for your emotions or choices. It is only you who holds the power to decide how you will respond and what you will feel in each moment.

One of my earliest childhood memories remains unclear to me—I'm not sure if it's a true memory, a dream, or a vision created by my mind. But as I mentioned before, whether it's a dream or a vision, it still holds truth. There is no timeline; we are, in essence, living within a dream.

I was sitting in the TV room, and I believe it was evening since my father had just come home from work. My mother and both sisters were sitting together, watching TV. I remember sitting in the corner near the TV, not paying attention to the programme. I had my toys scattered around me and spoke as if I were conversing with an invisible person.

I said, "God, angels, I promise I will not lie in my life. I promise to do good, be good, and live a good life."

The question is, how did I, at just three years old, know about God? Why was I saying such words? My immediate family wasn't particularly religious, so I couldn't have learnt it from my environment. This memory has stayed with me throughout my life. For many years, I didn't understand why I said those words, but as I gained more life experience and came to know my soul, I began to understand the invisible source that is available to us once we become conscious and awakened.

Throughout my life, there have been many moments when situations arose that, at the time, felt sorrowful and caused me suffering. However, as time passed and I gained more experience through hardship, I learnt that in every situation, we have a choice in how we perceive it. I have come to see each experience as part of a bigger picture, as a lesson, a play where I, as a soul, observe and analyse the unfolding events. I have learnt to recognise that it is just a play, just a test, and ultimately, just a dream.

This is not to say that I didn't react to some situations. However, even when I did, I realised that each reaction was a lesson, one that showed me that reacting isn't always necessary. The only outcome of reacting is suffering within yourself. I've learnt not to give weight to emotions that stem from the ego. I've come to understand that everything is temporary, and nothing lasts forever. The key is to navigate each challenge as best as you can. What does this mean? It means I've learnt to replace my reactions with a deeper understanding, bringing me closer to my higher self, my soul, my guardians, the universe, and God.

I have learnt that it's best to replace anger with compassion, fear with trust, sadness with hope, and hate with love. Throughout this book, we will explore the deeper meaning behind these shifts and discover how to transform fleeting emotions into lasting peace.

I feel incredibly fortunate to have reached a place in life where these words flow so effortlessly. I am grateful for the experiences that have challenged my soul and shaped my journey. It's a privilege to share these insights with you, with the hope that they may resonate and assist others. I do not take credit for these words, as they are born from the experiences the universe has provided. Therefore, I credit this book to the universe.

In this book, I have created characters to illustrate the various experiences that life can bring—whether they lead to light or darkness. Some of these stories are drawn from my own life, while others come from the experiences of those I have encountered. Ultimately, we are all tools, vessels for our higher selves, meant to bring greater good to this earth.

Chapter 1
Journey

Child – Development – Adult

When we are born, we arrive in this world as infants, beginning our journey on earth. Over time, we grow into adults, eventually ageing and eventually departing from this world. Some may have a shorter journey, while others may take longer. We can think of our life as a bridge: we enter from one side and depart from the other.

What truly matters is how we navigate this journey. How do you cross the bridge of life? The power to shape that journey lies more in your hands than you may realise.

As babies, we are innocent and pure, with no preconceived personality.

We love everything, find joy in everything, and offer love unconditionally. We are born with a soul untouched, in its true, perfect state.

We are born into families, though sometimes we are not. However, we choose not to say 'unfortunately' when a child has no family, because it truly does not matter. We are who we are, regardless of where we are born, our race, nationality, social status, or health. We are all souls within human bodies, each on our unique journey across the bridge of life. Ultimately, we are the ones who guide ourselves through it.

As we travel along our journey, we connect with other souls, but it is essential to remember that this journey is uniquely ours. Some souls may come together to fulfil a shared purpose, while others walk their path alone. There are also souls whose journeys require the support of many. The oldest souls are often the most enlightened, and they may have a twin soul that joins them on earth. Together, they unite to fulfil a greater mission, using their combined light to make a profound impact. This will be explored further later in the book.

Throughout our journey, we face the choice of walking in the light or the dark. As mentioned earlier, every child is born with a pure heart and inner light. So, what causes some to stray from this light as they grow? Why do some choose darkness over light? And what allows others to maintain their connection to the light throughout their lives?

It is the ego, the mind, that shapes our identity and guides us through the physical world. Some people learn to understand and manage their minds, allowing them to stay aligned with their soul's journey. Others, however, allow the ego to take control, leading them down a path focused on material pursuits.

Our ego begins to form in childhood and strengthens as we grow into adulthood. Through our interactions with others and our environment, we develop the identity we carry as humans. However, it's important to remember that the soul remains unchanged. The soul has no personality—only purity, love, kindness, and joy. This is our true essence. But when the ego grows stronger, the mind becomes preoccupied, often making it difficult to remember our soul's true nature.

In this chapter, we will explore how the ego develops, dividing the process into three stages: childhood, development (from adolescence to mid-life), and adulthood. Each stage plays a significant role in shaping the ego.

Child

For clarity, we will focus on a child raised within a family. The main character, known as Character 1, will guide us through the journey. Throughout this book, we will follow their life from childhood to development and into adulthood. As we delve into her experiences, we will examine how their ego formed and how they navigated life's challenges. Other characters will also appear along the way, but the focus will remain on Character 1's evolution.

As a baby, they were like many others—happy, joyful, and free from any personality or emotional baggage that comes with the development of the ego. This is the pure and innocent nature of a child from birth until they begin to grow older.

A year or two pass, and they begin to form the early stages of their personality. This developing personality is influenced by their surroundings—the environment in which they are raised. The reality of their household, the place of birth, and the country they grew up in during their early years all play a significant role in shaping who they become. Where we are born is important, as each country carries its unique energy. Older countries, which have experienced more pain throughout history, tend to have a collective 'pain body'—an energy that impacts its residents. Children born in such countries may feel this painful energy more acutely, especially those with older souls who are more attuned to it.

Now, they come from a wealthy family, so there are no issues with fulfilling their material needs. They also have a loving family, but much of their time is spent alone, surrounded by toys and an imaginary friend, as all family members are too busy to be present. Despite this, they adapt quickly and learn to find happiness within the environment they have created for themselves.

A few years pass, and they become a little older. Now, they have developed a stronger sense of personality, with an ego of their own. They begin attending school and making friends. At this stage, their reality expands beyond the family, and they start to see the world and experience it through their eyes. They begin absorbing new energies—some of which will stay with them throughout their lives, while others will fade away as life progresses.

As time passes, they begin to make choices based on their preferences—deciding what they like and what makes them happiest. This process becomes more prominent as their ego becomes more established. Over the years, their connections with other children have deepened. This is where the complexity of ego formation begins to unfold. Each child has their unique personality, shaped by the individual reality created within their household, which then expands outward into the world beyond.

The Ego comes into Play

Like most other children, they are a happy and joyful kid, full of energy and curiosity. However, unexpectedly, the sudden death of a parent marks a turning point in their early journey. This is the first test they face, arriving at just seven years old. At this age, they know nothing of the sadness that accompanies loss. All they have ever known is joy and happiness. They have never discussed death and loss, so this concept feels completely foreign to them.

This emotion is completely unfamiliar to them. Though their family tries to shield them by saying their father has gone abroad for work and will return someday, they sense something is wrong. The words don't feel truthful to them. They feel a deep sense of something missing, and a quiet voice within them tells them their father isn't coming back. Pain begins to form in their chest, and they feel a lump in their throat. Their bodies ache all over. They don't understand what these sensations mean, but they know something has changed.

They ask their mother, "Is he gone forever?"

The mother replies, "No, that's not true."

However, her voice and body language speak a different truth. As she answers, she places her hand on her throat – a sign of fear – and her voice trembles. Tears well up in her eyes. In that moment, the mother is caught in her emotional turmoil, feeling helpless. Unknowingly, the child steps into a more mature role.

With compassion, they comfort their mother, saying, "It's ok, if he's not coming back. I'm not upset; don't worry; I'm ok."

The mother, overwhelmed with emotion, breaks down in tears and embraces them. This moment marks a shift in their relationship, one that is forever changed.

So, when they said they were ok, were they truly ok? The answer depends on whether those words came from their ego or their higher self. If it came from their higher self, then yes, they are truly ok. They understand that their father is not really gone—only his physical body has departed. The soul remains eternal.

However, if those words came from their ego, the ego would not agree with this truth. As we will see, their ego will begin to generate emotions that will affect their well-being. Only if their higher self had been stronger at that moment could it have overshadowed the ego. But at that time, their higher self was not fully developed—it was still on the journey, one that had only just begun. This moment marked their first lesson in the journey of consciousness.

Their ego learns early on that it's best to hide their feelings, both to protect those around them and to shield themselves. At that moment, their main concern becomes protecting their mother and themselves. They attend school, but their confidence has vanished. They feel lost, unsure of what they truly feel.

The only thing they know is: *I must not show my emotions; I must be strong; I must smile.* And yes, they smile, but behind each smile lies a tear in their heart.

This internal conflict becomes the belief: *I'm not important,* or *I'm not ok.* Without realising it, suffering begins to shape their emotions. It is the ignorance of their true feelings that leads to the suppression of their radiant soul. The ego only takes control and creates the illusion of suffering when the soul ignores these emotions.

Ignorance of one's feelings is like placing a lid on boiling water—over time, the pressure builds, and eventually, it will explode.

If Awakened

If they had been awakened, they would have acknowledged their experience, their pain, and their loss. They would have returned to their higher self and listened, understanding that it is ok for their father to be gone, but it is also ok to feel pain. By acknowledging their emotions, they could then analyse them, face them, and learn from them. The next time such emotions arose, they would know that while the emotion exists, they don't have to suffer from it. This process isn't achieved through ignorance but through facing the emotion and embracing the lessons it brings.

By facing their emotions, their higher self would have come through more clearly, allowing them to find space to listen to the wisdom of their soul. They would have realised that their father had fulfilled his purpose in this life, and his soul was now at peace.

They would have understood, saying, "I am ok, and mother is ok. She is simply going through a natural human emotion."

They would have known that if they wished to connect with their father, they could, as souls are always able to connect at any given time. This is what it means to understand the situation, trust the universe, let go of the ego, and dive deep into the connection of souls. It's about living fully in the present moment.

If their mother had been awakened, they wouldn't have felt the need to hide the truth about their father's passing, believing that shielding them from reality would protect them both from pain. In doing so, their mother unknowingly created an emotional barrier for herself, having to pretend and act in front of them. A wiser approach would have been to be honest with them, face the situation as it was, and work together to find a way to cope. By doing this, the situation could have shifted, allowing space for the higher self to offer clarity and healing.

Exercise

Given the example above, write down the earliest emotion that you experienced in your childhood that brought you unsatisfaction or sorrow. After writing the analysis, did you ignore it, or did you face it?

If you ignored it, what emotions did it bring to you?

If you faced it, what emotions did it bring to you?

Development

The teenage years, often referred to as the development stage, are a crucial part of our lives. These years are typically a source of concern for many parents, and understandably so. Why? These are the years characterised by confusion and inner turmoil, as teenagers strive to define themselves. It is during this stage that we begin to form and solidify the voice of our ego. We start to question which version of ourselves we want to express, what role we want to play in the material world, and what kind of relationships we seek. The search for identity becomes central, and the list of questions and choices seems endless.

A seemingly confused teenager is often someone who is in the process of searching for their soul's purpose. Of course, this search can lead down different paths. Some may find their way to enlightenment eventually, while others might experience years of suffering before reaching that point—or in some cases, they may never find it at all. On the other hand, a teenager who does not exhibit confusion and simply follows their parents' directives without question may be an individual who is not yet on a path of self-discovery. It's likely that later in life, during a midlife crisis or a period of introspection, they will embark on their journey to find deeper meaning and understanding on their terms.

A midlife crisis can be seen as another phase of development—a moment when you reassess your place in the world, especially if you haven't awakened to your true self before this time. Positions, status, and material accomplishments belong to the ego, not to your soul. If you are deeply connected with your soul, there would be no need for a breakdown or a midlife crisis, because you would already know that true fulfilment comes from within, not from external validation.

At a young age, they learnt to suppress their emotions and simply navigate life as it came. However, as time passed, they began to observe other emotional experiences—not from within themselves, but from their family. Their mother became deeply depressed. As a result, she withdrew emotionally and paid little attention to them. Her depression stemmed from the loss of her husband, the challenges of raising them as a single mother, and the financial struggles that followed.

Once again, they suppress their emotions, seeking refuge in playing with toys and imaginary friends. They learn that the best way to cope with difficult situations is to disconnect and immerse themselves in the happiness of the world they've created in their imagination. In doing so, they unknowingly begin to walk the path toward enlightenment—embracing the present moment. They reassure themselves that this is only temporary and that it will pass.

As they enter their teenage years, curiosity begins to stir within them, prompting deep questions about the meaning of life. They wonder why they are here on earth, why they were born into their family, and why their thoughts often differ from those of those around them. The questions keep piling up—why, and why, and why?

At the age of 16, they decide to take control of their own reality. They begin seeking ways to become independent and understand the deeper meaning behind their existence. Eager to embark on their personal journey, they set out to uncover life's purpose. However, there's a flaw in their approach: in their quest for meaning, they distance themselves from their family and unknowingly harbour anger towards them, blaming them for the pain and struggles they've endured.

If Awakened

Had they awakened at that time, they would have felt empathy for their family. Rather than retreating into their world, they would have reached out to support their mother, lifting her spirits. If they had been awakened, they would have chosen compassion over anger and understanding over blame, recognising that their family were also navigating their struggles.

No one else is responsible for your emotions or your journey. When you place blame, you are merely trying to shift responsibility for your actions.

onto someone else. You are the only one who can control the experiences you choose to invite or reject in your life.

Exercise

Think of the situation in your teenage years that you decided to do that brought you the adulthood life.

Now think: if you were awakened, would you have made the same decision?

Adult

Your adult years will unfold depending on whether you've already awakened to your purpose or if that realisation comes later. If you are awake, you know what you want from this life, and you'll channel all your energy into fulfilling the purpose of your existence. If not, you may find yourself merely passing the time, unaware that there's a deeper purpose you're meant to fulfil. Eventually, this realisation will come, and when it does, you may experience a mid-life crisis—this can happen at any age when you realise you're not living in alignment with your true calling.

If they don't awaken, they will carry the anger and blame from their teenage years into adulthood, projecting these emotions onto others. They will unconsciously attract people who mirror the dynamics of their family, continuing to direct their unresolved feelings toward them, almost as if seeking revenge.

However, if they awaken, they will find peace within themselves, tuning into the voice inside and learning to trust the universe and its messages. They will let go of past hurts and embrace the present, finding joy in each moment.

Exercise

Are you satisfied with the position you have as an adult?
If yes, explain why.
If no, explain why.

Have your childhood and teenage years left a scar on your emotions? Write down the emotions and whom you blame.

Now write down can whether you can forgive them or not, And what if you got rid of these emotions? How do you think you would benefit from it?

Suffering

Suffering is a word most known to be used by Buddha. It is born with set of emotions that belongs to the ego. We bring suffering to our being, not anyone or anything else.

The root of suffering lies in emotions such as anger, greed, lies, deceit, attachment, and many others, which create emotional pain and can eventually manifest as physical discomfort. The soul, however, is unfamiliar with the concept of suffering. It is grounded in true love, kindness, forgiveness, peace, contentment, and courage.

The sooner we connect with our souls, the sooner we are free from suffering. Connecting with your soul means connecting with God, the universe, and the universal energy. Once this connection is made, you realise that you are safe, strong, and capable of achieving great things, ultimately serving humanity. There is nothing more powerful than the creator of this world, and the way to connect with that power is through your soul.

Being awakened doesn't mean you won't face obstacles on this earth—because you will. It's a natural part of being here, meant to help you learn and grow. Some face more challenges, while others face fewer. However, when you are awakened, you learn to navigate each situation with wisdom, and no experience will have the power to make you suffer. You begin to accept, embrace, learn, and apply the lessons that life presents, allowing each moment to contribute to your growth.

Remember, suffering doesn't only arise from unfortunate events. It can emerge even when life seems perfect. When you're not awakened, you may find yourself constantly thinking about wanting more or fearing the loss of what you already have. This mindset creates a sense of unrest, preventing you from fully embracing the present moment.

An ego that thrives on suffering brings darkness into our lives, dimming the light of our beautiful souls. In the next chapter, we will explore the emotions created by the ego, presenting a series of stories to analyse how each situation might unfold when faced with an awakened soul. These stories will illustrate how individuals can unknowingly create darkness in their lives and highlight how simple it can be to avoid falling into the traps the ego sets.

To connect with the soul, one must transcend the ego, as the ego lowers our vibration and obscures the light within. Every action we take should serve the soul, and by consciously choosing what nourishes us, we invite light and happiness into our lives. The more we align with our true essence, the more we see the light and feel inner joy. When you are awakened, you always know.

Darkness (created by our ego)

"We are all beautiful souls, children of God. There is no such thing as a bad soul. When someone acts in a way that harms others, it is simply the ego at play, a disconnect from the divine guidance of the soul. It is not their fault; they simply need guidance and unconditional love."

"Consciousness is about being in harmony with our soul, allowing the light within us to shine. If one fails to connect with their soul, they live in confusion, which persists until they learn to trust the invisible power that is a gift to them. Once they do, they can fulfil the purpose they were given as a human on this earth, and upon completion, they will return home in peace."

"Do not become a prisoner of your thoughts, nor allow others to imprison you in theirs. Be the light that empowers and enlightens those around you."

Enlightenment is a blessing that recognises no darkness. In every situation, there is an inner light. An awakened soul understands that every experience is here to teach us a lesson, and as a result, all situations bring blessings.

Darkness can take many forms. As mentioned in the previous chapter, it can arise from situations like loss, death, or war. However, darkness can also emerge even when none of these appear. If your soul is asleep, you will experience suffering, even if life seems 'perfect'. This suffering manifests through emotions and actions such as greed, fear, ungratefulness, lying, cheating, and stealing.

The phrase 'there is a light at the end of the tunnel' is often used, but the more accurate way to express it is 'there is a light within the tunnel'.

This is because it is our perception that shapes how we feel and what we experience throughout our journey on this earth.

There are situations created by humans, such as war, conflict, arguments, bullying, lies, cheating, manipulation, and theft. Then, there are natural events that unfold, like death, illness, and accidents. While we can't always control these occurrences, we can control how we respond to them. Although we can't control our external environment, we do have control over our own lives. By learning to navigate these challenges without suffering, we not only find peace but also become equipped to help others do the same.

Why do we even label actions that stem from human behaviours? In certain ways, these labels may incite individuals to either embrace these behaviours or perceive them as their own. In contrast, words like love, empathy, compassion, harmony, and kindness hold far greater significance. They transcend mere words—they bring light to our beings and uplift our spirits.

If we learn from an early age that each person is a soul and that the ego is responsible for the emotions that cause suffering, we can better understand how to interact with those who are not yet awakened.

For instance, if you find yourself thinking, *I'm being bullied,* it's important to recognise that this is an illusion created by your ego. The ego feeds on fear and seeks to perpetuate it, often attracting such behaviours. On the other hand, someone who engages in bullying is displaying weakness. Their ego thrives on exerting power over others, but deep down, they are crying for help. In these moments, let your light shine with compassion, understanding, and love, offering healing to both you and others.

The person who feels they are being bullied should find the courage to let go of their fear and instead offer help to the other person. Remember, the one who is bullying is operating from a place of weakness. By offering comfort and support, you provide them with the strength they need, and in doing so, you guide them towards a path of light and healing.

If you feel the urge to bully someone to make yourself feel stronger, resist that temptation. Instead, set aside your insecurities and choose to empower the other person. By helping them become fearless, you gain true strength, and in doing so, create a win-win situation for both of you.

What is war? War is the ego's craving for power and greed. We are all one, and we should not let race, religion, gender, or nationality divide us.

Now, let's explore both emotions that arise from the ego and examine what happens when you are awakened.

Emotions

It is essential to recognise and understand our negative emotions. Some may experience only a few, while others may struggle with many. This is known as the 'shadow self'—the darker side of our personality. Without acknowledging and understanding our shadow self, we cannot truly know ourselves.

Many people confuse the concept of negative emotions. For example, if someone smiles at you, speaks kindly, and appears positive on the outside but is secretly manipulating or lying, that behaviour is negative. On the other hand, if someone doesn't smile but has good intentions toward you, that is not negative. Negativity is about the intention behind a person's actions, not just what is shown on the surface. This misunderstanding is a common source of confusion when it comes to the term 'negative'.

To gain control over your own emotions and to better understand the intentions of others, it is essential to familiarise yourself with each emotion. This awareness serves as the gateway to freeing yourself from their influence.

Exercise

Before we look into these emotions in depth

Write down negative emotions that you may think you have.

Then write down a negative emotion from others that has affected you in your life.

Anger

People with a hot temper do foolish things; wiser people remain calm *(Proverbs 14:17)*.

Buddha

Holding on to anger is like grasping a hot coal with the intent of throwing it at someone else; you are the one who gets burnt.

Anger is a negative emotion rooted in the ego, as the soul is too compassionate to generate such feelings. Blame, frustration, and unforgiveness are often associated with it. Those who tend to blame others often express their emotions through anger, and the same applies to frustration and the inability to forgive, both of which can trigger anger within us.

When someone wrongs us, we have a choice: to respond with forgiveness and compassion or to hold onto anger and resentment. The decision is ours alone.

The difference lies in the path we choose. If we opt for anger and resentment, we not only harm ourselves but also cause pain to the other person. In doing so, we miss the opportunity to learn from the experience and inadvertently discourage the other from reconnecting with their true self.

On the other hand, if we choose the path of forgiveness and compassion, our hearts will feel liberated, and our souls will be filled with gratitude for the lesson presented to us. This choice allows us to grow and move closer to enlightenment while also guiding the other person to reconnect with their true self. Deep down, no one genuinely desires to harm others—they are simply unaware, caught in a slumber of the soul. At their core, everyone carries goodness within them.

Exercise

Think of an example from your past when you felt this emotion. What was the reason for your anger? And how did you deal with it? What was the result?

And if you were awakened, what do you think you would have done differently and from there what result do you think you would have got instead?

Now give another example of your past when someone else got angry with you. What was the reason? And how did you deal with it? What was the result?

And if you were awakened, do you think it would have been different?

<u>Jealousy</u>
James 3:14-15
But if you have bitter jealousy and selfish ambition in your hearts, do not boast and be false to the truth. This is not the wisdom that comes down from above but is earthly, unspiritual, demonic.

Buddha

Don't ruin other people's happiness just because you can't find your own.

Jealousy is a negative emotion that arises when you envy someone else's life or possessions, desiring what they have. But ask yourself—do you truly want what they have? Why not focus on creating your unique path, which will bring you far greater fulfilment? Jealousy can linger with a person from childhood to old age. Even when they have everything they've ever wished for, they may still find reasons to envy something another person has or does. It is an emotion rooted in dissatisfaction and a disconnect from appreciating one's blessings and potential.

Jealousy is one of the most painful and shadowed states of being, often serving as a primary source of deep suffering.

A lack of gratitude for one's own life often drives a person to seek validation externally. Even when they possess everything they once wished for, they remain unsatisfied and crave more. This dissatisfaction leads them to envy others' lives, desiring what others have—even if it's not aligned with their true desires. This mindset stems from greed and an inability to appreciate the blessings they already have. Over time, it fosters deeper unhappiness and ushers them into a dark emotional state. It's a place of division, disconnecting them from inner peace and harmony.

A person who embraces gratitude lives in a state of contentment and peace, fully appreciating the blessings the universe has provided. This mindset fosters even greater joy when witnessing another's happiness or success, as they view it not as separate from their own but as a shared experience of unity. The joy of another person becomes their own, mirroring the reality of our interconnectedness. This perspective represents a state of enlightenment—a place of oneness and harmony with all of existence.

Dishonesty

Proverbs 12:22
The Lord detests lying lips, but he delights in people who are trustworthy.

Buddha

Three things cannot be long hidden: the sun, the moon, and the truth.

A lie can range from something seemingly minor, like claiming, 'I woke up at 7 a.m.', when the truth is they woke up at noon but felt embarrassed to admit it, to something far more significant, such as denying responsibility for stealing a necklace, saying, "It wasn't me," when, in reality, it was them, and the lie serves to avoid returning it.

Dishonesty can manifest in seemingly harmless forms or more overtly harmful ways. Regardless of whether a lie is small or significant, both undermine the integrity of the soul.

Every lie, no matter how small, casts a shadow over your pure soul, dimming the light that shines within. While others may never discover your falsehoods, the most profound impact is that you carry the weight of that dishonesty within yourself.

Manipulation

Matthew 7:15

'Beware of false prophets, who come to you in sheep's clothing but inwardly are ravenous wolves'.

This emotion is closely tied to harmful lies and selfishness, as it drives one to achieve their desires through the manipulation of others.

This behaviour can provide a false sense of power to an ego that has learnt to manipulate others to achieve its desires. However, it is far more destructive than it appears. This pattern of behaviour feeds an insatiable drive, creating a cycle that perpetuates harm – to others and oneself – in an endless pursuit of selfish goals.

This behaviour reflects a lack of faith and trust in the universe's ability to provide what is truly meant for us. Pursuing what is not aligned with our path may offer temporary satisfaction, but it will ultimately leave us unfulfilled. On the other hand, embracing faith and trusting that what is meant for us will come brings lasting contentment. This mindset unlocks a flow of abundance and miracles, guiding us toward a life of true purpose and joy.

We have little control over what destiny has in store for us. What we can cultivate, however, is the courage and strength to embrace truth and remain attentive to the signs along our journey. By tuning into these signals, we can sense if we are on the right path. If it feels aligned, we can dedicate our energy wholeheartedly, trusting that with the universe's guidance and support, we will arrive where we are meant to be.

Attachments

"Attachment is the source of all suffering." – Buddha.

Attachment manifests in many forms and is a deeply rooted emotional behaviour that often leads to significant suffering. Other challenging emotions often accompany it, resulting in a cycle of pain and longing. The weight of attachment brings endless struggles, yet it is a burden many humans willingly carry.

What is attachment? It can range from the smallest, fleeting connections to overwhelming, all-consuming bonds. Attachment can manifest toward people, wealth, power, or material possessions—all things tied to this earthly existence.

If you are attached to a person – be it a family member, partner, or friend – what happens if they leave, whether due to natural causes or a personal decision? How will your attachment serve you then? If you have a strong attachment to wealth, contemplate the potential consequences of facing bankruptcy or losing everything as a result of poor decisions. How will you cope? If your attachment is to power – say, as the head of a multimillion-pound company – and that power vanishes in the blink of an eye due to a stock market crash, what will you do? Or if your attachment lies in earthly possessions, such as deriving joy from music, and you suddenly lose your hearing in an accident, how will you find peace?

Will you spend years trying to heal? Will you ever truly heal? Will you resort to emotions like anger, disappointment, resentment, or depression to fill the void? Such responses will only deepen your suffering and prolong your pain.

Love without attachment. Live without attachment. Breathe without attachment. Experience everything fully, yet freely, without clinging. Let your soul soar unbound, for attachment is merely another name for the soul's imprisonment.

Gossiping

James 4:11

Do not speak evil against one another, brothers. The one who speaks against a brother or judges his brother, speaks evil against the law and judges the law. But if you judge the law, you are not a doer of the law but a judge.

Buddha

What is evil? Killing is evil, lying is evil, slandering is evil, abuse is evil, gossip is evil, envy is evil, hatred is evil, to cling to false doctrine is evil; all these things are evil. And what is the root of evil? Desire is the root of evil, illusion is the root of evil.

A behaviour that serves no purpose other than wasting precious time on this earth. This world is a school, and we must use our time wisely to learn the lessons we are meant to learn and fulfil our tasks to the best of our ability.

Gossiping has become a form of entertainment for many people. It serves to pastime, but ultimately it is a waste of time. Like many other behaviours, gossiping can vary in intensity, ranging from small remarks to much larger, more harmful conversations.

Gossiping often stems from a lack of courage to speak the truth. Fear of being honest can lead people to avoid direct communication and instead share the information with others. If we had the courage to face the person directly and tell them the truth, we wouldn't waste time talking about it with others.

The truth is a powerful and beautiful energy, freely available to all. By embracing it, we can free ourselves and others.

Anxiety

Philippians 4:6-7

1. Do not be anxious about anything, but in every situation, by prayer and petition, with thanksgiving, present your requests to God.
2. And the peace of God, which transcends all understanding, will guard your hearts and your minds in Christ Jesus.

Anxiety is one of the most common emotions experienced by humans in our daily lives. Some individuals experience it more intensely, while others feel it less. Some can manage it with natural remedies, while others rely on medications to control it. Unfortunately, for some who struggle to manage this emotion, it can lead to self-medication with substances – whether legal medications or alcohol – which can harm their bodies over time.

Anxiety can arise from both small and significant situations in our lives. It is closely linked to fear—the internal worry about what might happen. It is also a twin to overthinking, a mental battle where we get caught up in thoughts of the past and future, often losing sight of the beauty of the present moment, which holds the true peace we seek.

Why do we experience such an emotion? Is it possible to eliminate it for good? The answer is yes, it is possible.

Those who have faith and trust in the divine understand, deep down, that everything unfolds in divine timing. Everything happens as it should. The divine light is always there to protect your life and your journey. Embracing this truth quiets the emotions of anxiety. This awareness is a form of enlightenment and a deep connection with the universe.

Fear

Psalm 118:6-7
The Lord is with me; I will not be afraid. What can man do to me? The Lord is with me; he is my helper.

Buddha

'Even death is not to be feared by one who has lived wisely'.

Fear arises when we lack faith and struggle to trust the universe. It reflects uncertainty and doubt, showing a disconnect from the deeper flow of life.

Like anxiety, fear is an emotion that transforms into energy, flowing through our minds and manifesting in our bodies. In some cases, fear is simply a mental illusion, while in others, it reflects real circumstances. Regardless, we can learn to release fear and approach each situation with a positive mindset.

Fear, especially when it's based on illusion, can hinder our progress as human beings. Our parents often teach us this emotion from a very young age. For example, if a parent expresses fear that we might burn ourselves by touching fire, we absorb this emotion and carry it with us, often applying it later in our own lives.

When one has faith and trust, they know they are always protected by a higher source of energy. With this deep trust, fear cannot enter their life for long; if it does, it will quickly dissipate, unable to withstand the strength of their inner light. This light is enlightenment—an unwavering reminder of the power within that nothing can harm unless you allow it. Keep your light shining, for it is your ultimate protector.

Cheating

Matthew 5:27-28

"You have heard that it was said, 'You shall not commit adultery'. But I say to you that everyone who looks at a woman with lustful intent has already committed adultery with her in his heart.

"Cheating others or yourself is ultimately a betrayal of your own soul. By doing so, you limit the space for your soul

to grow, as you fill it with memories of guilt and regret that hinder your progress."

Cheating manifests in various forms—whether in romantic relationships, exam rooms, or business dealings. At its core, it is a behavioural dysfunction driven by the desire to avoid hard work, evade the truth, or gain power to feed the ego.

When one is awakened, they align themselves with the path chosen by the divine. This path grants them access to a deep, indescribable knowing—an inner wisdom that guides them. In this state, there is no need to cheat or deceive, for they already know what they want and how to attain it, using the universal knowledge and wisdom they possess.

When one awakens in romantic life, they recognise their true soulmate—their twin soul, the one divinely intended for them. This relationship is not only a partnership but also a deep friendship and a sense of home. They are you in a different body, and you cannot cheat on yourself, nor would you ever want to. You unite in trust and peace, realising that they are you and you are them. It is the pure beauty of oneness, home, a reflection of enlightenment and light.

When you walk your path of light, cheating has no place. You are on the path of true power, of heaven, and of enlightenment.

Grudge

Matthew 6:14-15

For if you forgive others their trespasses, your heavenly Father will also forgive you, but if you do not forgive others their trespasses, neither will your Father forgive your trespasses.

Buddha

"Holding onto anger is like drinking poison and expecting the other person to die."

"Holding a grudge is like imprisoning your soul; it is you, not anyone else, who will suffer the most from holding onto it."

A grudge is the opposite of forgiveness and living in the present moment. It is one of the most powerful emotions, driven by a strong ego. When you hold a grudge, you effectively block yourself from moving forward, keeping you tethered to a past situation that no longer serves you.

This emotion can linger with a person indefinitely, or one can choose to let go of it, allowing themselves to move forward and heal.

There can be no grudge when there is understanding, forgiveness, and empathy. These are the keys that unlock the universal light, bringing enlightenment and peace.

Greed

Luke 12:15

Then he said to them, "Watch out! Be on your guard against all kinds of greed; life does not consist in an abundance of possessions."

Buddha

Greed is an imperfection that defiles the mind; hate is an imperfection that defiles the mind; delusion is an imperfection that defiles the mind.

"Greed is the root of suffering. Save your soul before it's too late. Take control before it's too late, for greed will never cease its endless craving and will drain your soul until nothing remains."

Greed arises from dissatisfaction, a constant yearning for more, no matter how much you have. The more you acquire, the more you desire, creating an endless cycle of longing. This doesn't mean you shouldn't have ambition or work toward greater goals, but rather that you should appreciate what you already have and pursue your aspirations without falling into dissatisfaction or greed. These emotions only lead to suffering.

The phrase 'If I have that, I will be happy and satisfied' reveals that you are giving yourself an excuse to delay happiness, waiting for something external to make you feel fulfilled. This cycle will never end, because once you obtain what you believe will bring happiness, you'll find something else to desire, and the wait for contentment will continue indefinitely. True happiness comes from embracing the present moment, not from waiting for external circumstances to change.

Hopeless

Jeremiah 29:11

"For I know the plans I have for you," declares the Lord, *"plans for welfare and not for evil, to give you a future and hope."*

Do not lose hope, as hope is the fruit of your soul – TG.

Being hopeless is a deep dark place. This comes in different degrees, could be mild and could be severe.

A mild would be a situation that brings a hopeless feeling that makes you feel down, and then some time will pass and you will be able to bring yourself up again. Then a different degree would be mild depression which could be sorted by activities or by a mild medical drug. Then it goes higher, a depression that is not temporary but a lifetime depression that has to be sorted by more serious medical drugs. And then we all know what severe could be thinking of hurting yourself or, even worse suicide.

Knowing what belongs to you, and giving away what is not yours is the key to shining light to greed. What is meant to be yours will be yours.

Judgement

Luke 6:37

Do not judge others, and you will not be judged. Do not condemn others, or it will all come back against you. Forgive others, and you will be forgiven.

Buddha

Do not be the judge of people; do not make assumptions about others. A person is destroyed by holding judgements about others.

"I choose not to judge myself or you, for we are both enough, and we are all connected as one. Rather than judging, I embrace compassion."

This emotion stems from a sense of separation from others. It is a product of a strong and deeply entrenched ego, which thrives and grows stronger through the act of judging others.

Judging others often originates from past experiences, such as learning this behaviour from a parent or authority figure during childhood. Alternatively, it may arise as a defence mechanism to shield feelings of low self-esteem. Regardless of its origin, judging others ultimately brings suffering to yourself, not to the person being judged. In most cases, your judgements have little to no impact on the other person; instead, you carry the emotional weight of this habit, burdening your well-being.

Judgemental tendencies can vary in intensity, ranging from mild to severe. If your tendencies are mild, take time to reflect and explore the underlying reasons for this behaviour. If they are severe, you might be less inclined to engage with this chapter, but if you are, know that it is never too late to address and transform this behavioural pattern. With effort and awareness, even deeply ingrained tendencies can be shifted toward healthier and more compassionate ways of being.

When we recognise that we are all interconnected and share the same journey, we gain a deeper understanding that the actions or inactions of others reflect our own. We are one consciousness, and as we let go of judging others, we also liberate ourselves from self-judgement, moving closer to true freedom and inner peace.

This realisation brings us one step closer to enlightenment—free, radiant, and united, as one light.

Conclusion

We have now examined the emotions and behaviours that do not serve the greater good of humanity. If, at any point in life, you act in a way influenced by darkness, know that you are forgiven by God the moment you seek forgiveness. Why? Because in the eyes of God and the universe, there is no such concept as darkness—this is a construct created by humans, shaped by the mind. The very act of recognising your misstep is already a step toward forgiveness and redemption.

The reason is that through the simple act of recognition, you are turning toward the light. While it is wise to seek forgiveness from God, the universe, and those you may have hurt, this act of humility and accountability brings you one step closer to aligning with your soul.

An apology must come from within, genuine and heartfelt. Offering an apology for personal gain or to further manipulate a situation is not a true apology—it is insincere. A real apology arises from the heart, free of ulterior motives. When you apologise to another person, it should be unconditional, with no expectation of reward or acknowledgement in return. True apologies are acts of humility.

A sincere apology comes from the heart and soul, not just from the surface. While 'apology' is merely a word, its true value lies in its origin—whether it arises from the ego or the soul. An apology rooted in the ego is superficial, often driven by appearance rather than growth, and may lead to repeated patterns of the same behaviour. Conversely, an apology that springs from the soul reflects true understanding and a genuine commitment to change. It indicates that one has learnt a lesson and will not repeat the behaviour. Remember, it is never too late to apologise. God is infinitely forgiving, and through the act of seeking forgiveness, you open yourself to growth and learning.

Being Awakened

Throughout this book, we often discuss the concept of awakening. But what does it truly mean? Why is it called awakening? How do we become awakened? Does it only come through suffering? These are just some of the questions that may arise as we explore the deeper meaning of awakening.

In simple terms, awakening means your soul stirs from within and reunites with the universe from which it originated. You become one with the cosmos, gaining the ability to understand its hidden language. Your soul aligns with the divine, feeling the power of God within. You begin to perceive the light surrounding your physical body, a protective energy that shields you from harm. Like a bird, you soar beyond the limits of your imagination, free and limitless.

Does awakening only occur through suffering? Not at all. While suffering is often a catalyst for awakening, as it overwhelms the mind with intense energies until it can no longer function, awakening can also happen without suffering. The key is a strong desire to awaken, a clear intention to quiet the mind, and the dedication to learn and practise this process. With discipline and commitment, you can master the art of stilling the mind and begin your journey of awakening without the need for suffering.

Being awakened means your soul breaking free from the confines of your human mind and ego. You reconnect with your true, childlike essence—unburdened by suffering. In this state, you begin to see the truth that has always been present, though your mind may have once blinded you to it. The truth is that the true beauty, blessing, and joy of life are all around you and within you, always. You don't need to search for it—it has always been there, from the moment you were born. You simply forgot it amidst the distractions and conditioning of human life.

A child who finds joy in the sight of a butterfly. The touch of the grass brings happiness to the child. The child finds significance in the shapes of the clouds. The child experiences a sense of hope upon witnessing the unification of two birds. A child whose heart is warmed by the sun on their skin. The child's imagination is boundless as they tally the stars.

We are all born with the inherent joy of life. To reconnect with our soul, we simply need to undo the layers we've learnt and cleanse ourselves. Life is beautiful, and God's unlimited power is available to us at any moment. To access it, we must align with our soul. Your soul is you—there is no need for soul searching, for you are already your soul. Quiet your mind and listen to it; it is the voice of your soul. You are a child of God, a creation of the divine, and an integral part of the universe.

This is the essence of awakening: returning to your pure soul, just as you were born to be—full of untainted happiness and joy.

Two ways to Look at Life

Life is full of situations that may not always be pleasant or kind. When such challenges arise, what can one do? How can we respond to make the situation better?

In life, there are always two ways to view any situation: from a descending or an ascending perspective. It's important to remember that everything happens for a reason, and when you release attachment, you can learn to see all situations from an upward, expansive viewpoint. When you have hope and trust in the power of the universe, no situation can seem greater than the strength you hold within. The truth, light, peace, and happiness reside within you, and no external circumstance can take that away.

You hold a unique power, and no one else can possess it. This power is nurtured by the greater force of God, charged through your belief and trust. Situations may come and go, but one thing that remains constant is you. When you believe and trust, nothing can stop your ascent, no matter how small or how great the challenges may be.

Create a Heaven

"We are the creators of our heaven or hell; we are the architects of our own lives."

Heaven is essentially a state of true happiness that comes from within—a deep, inner joy that is not dependent on the external world. It means that no matter the circumstances or situations you face, they do not disturb your inner peace. It's important to understand that this doesn't mean life won't present challenges—some mild, others more intense. However, by cultivating an awakened state of mind, we learn to navigate any situation with a sense of spaciousness within ourselves. Everything will pass, but what remains is you, and no external event should be able to disturb your inner equilibrium.

Heaven is a state of being—a space you create within yourself.

If you ask, "How do I create heaven?" it suggests that you have not yet awakened. A true state of being is the recognition that you are already in heaven. Heaven is you, your soul, your inner self—it is the light and peace within you. This state is not dependent on the fleeting happiness that life may bring. No other person can give you this state, though they may help nurture it. Ultimately, the source of this heaven resides within you.

Heaven is found in the ability to appreciate the smallest things in life. When you sit on your bed, gaze at the clouds, and feel a deep sense of joy within, you know you are awakened. If you wake in the morning and feel an extra surge of happiness as the light shines on your face, you are awakened. You are fully present, experiencing the moment without dwelling on the past or the future. In this state, your mind surrenders its power to your soul, the place where there are no boundaries. You are truly alive from within.

Towards the end, when my mother was in hospice, she was no longer allowed to go outside for walks or see the grass or the sky. I asked her, "Mom, is there anything I can do for you? What do you need?"

She replied, "All I want, all I wish for, is to be outside—to smell the grass, see the birds singing, watch the clouds, and feel the air on my skin."

I gently told her, "Mom, you can still be there. You can travel there with your soul."

The lesson here is that, in our busy lives, we often overlook the small details that make life beautiful. Don't wait until the end to learn to appreciate these simple joys. The sooner you learn, the sooner you experience heaven. No matter where you are, who you are, or what your circumstances may be, the beauty of the universe is always available to you, free of charge. It doesn't matter your country, religion, or social status—whether you're rich or poor. We are all one, and that is the true meaning of life. Embrace and enjoy this truth, for it is never too late.

The ego, on the other hand, feeds on emotions that cast a shadow over the heaven within you. While it's natural to experience emotions, the key is to feel them fully and then let them go. With practice, you may even reach a point where you no longer feel the need to hold onto these emotions. In the previous chapter, we explored the emotions that create darkness. Now, we will focus on the emotions that bring heaven into your being.

Humbleness

James 4:10
Humble yourselves before the Lord, and he will lift you.

Quran 25:63
And the slaves of God are those who walk on the earth in humility and calmness, and when the foolish address them (with bad words), they reply with mild words of gentleness.

Buddha
Never believe you are above or below anyone. Keep a humble spirit.

Humbleness is one of the greatest qualities a person can possess. It brings a sense of calm and inner peace, allowing you to let go of the need to prove yourself to others. Humbleness creates the space and freedom to act in alignment with what is best, without seeking recognition or validation. When you act with humbleness, it means your actions were not motivated by a desire for fame or popularity but by the intention to nourish your soul and others and contribute to the well-being of humanity.

Be genuine in everything you do, and as a result, you won't feel the need to boast about your accomplishments. It's the same with possessions—if you have more than others, there's no need to announce it. You don't need to feel superior. If you do, it means you're not at peace with yourself but in a constant battle to feel better than others. Instead, have, do, give, and remain quiet and humble about it. This will bring you true inner peace.

Hope

Romans 15:13

May the God of hope fill you with all joy and peace in believing, so that by the power of the Holy Spirit you may abound in hope.

"Hope is the essence of God within us—the boundless energy and light, an unlimited resource."

With hope, there are no limits to what we can achieve. It is like a powerful energy flowing through our being, awakening every cell and driving us to believe that anything is possible. Hope ignites a force within us, making the impossible seem attainable.

Great hope comes from the understanding that we are one with God and one with the universe. When we hold hope in our hearts, it signifies that we have been entrusted with a task that aligns with a higher purpose. By listening to this guidance, we can be certain that we will manifest what we hope for.

Everything is energy, everything is vibration, and everything is a power within us, fuelled by a higher source.

Hope makes your soul dance and flow with the universe, reminding you that you are never alone. It empowers you with the strength to achieve what may seem impossible.

Honesty

1 John 3:18

Dear children, let us not love with words or speech but with actions and in truth.

Buddha

Oh, how sweet it is to enjoy life, living in honesty and strength! And wisdom is sweet, and freedom.

"True peace and joy come from being honest with yourself and others."

Honesty is a powerful and virtuous quality. Being honest means staying true to yourself and others, knowing that there are always watchful eyes upon you—those of angels, of God. When you are honest, they see it; when you are not, they see that too.

When you're not honest, you can feel it in your gut—it slowly eats away at you from within. But when you embrace honesty, you rest with ease and comfort, knowing your soul is at peace. Honesty is one of the doorways to enlightenment, bringing you one step closer to a genuine, truthful relationship with a higher power.

One of my earliest memories of finding joy in honesty dates to when I was around three or four years old. Left to my own devices, I took pleasure in walking around the house with a bag in hand, collecting items that didn't belong to me from each room. By the end of the day, the bag was so heavy that I could barely carry it.

In the evenings, when everyone in the household would be gathered to watch TV, I would eagerly grab my bag and excitedly show what I had collected from each of their rooms. They would look at me with surprise, not understanding why I was showing them what I had done. Afterward, I would carefully return each item to its rightful owner, asking if they could take it with them.

This became my source of entertainment for about six months, I believe. One might wonder what the enjoyment was in that. Looking back, I realise the true joy came from discovering how honesty can bring such a sense of fulfilment. No one needed to know I had taken their things, and no one would have noticed, as the items I took were unused. I could have simply returned them without anyone ever finding out. But by choosing to take the items and then openly showing what I had done, I was embracing an act of honesty.

Another memory I have is from a time when I was travelling by coach. It was a period in my life when finances were tight, and the bus fare was £5. Back then, you would buy your ticket directly from the driver. I handed the driver a £10 note and waited for him to give me my ticket and change. He gave me both, and I made my way upstairs to find a seat. Upon opening my bag to deposit the change into my wallet, I discovered that I had received £15, not £5. The driver had mistakenly thought I'd given him £20. For a moment, my mind considered how I could use the extra £10 for something enjoyable. But almost instantly, I realised that the money didn't belong to me, and I needed to return it. I stood up, walked downstairs, and told the driver that he had given me too much change. I handed the extra £10 back to him. The look on his face at that moment gave me a sense of joy that no amount of money could ever buy. I was grateful that I listened to my soul and ignored the fleeting temptation of my mind.

Be honest, even when no one else is watching. You can see; your soul can see; your higher self can see; angels can see; and God can see.

Empathy

Romans 12:15

Rejoice with those who rejoice, weep with those who weep.

"Be a friend in both good times and bad. Be a steady rock that others can always rely on."

What a beautiful quality it is to be an empath. Being an empath is truly a doorway to the soul. It means putting yourself in another's shoes, and feeling what they feel. If they experience pain, you feel their pain. If they are happy, you share their joy.

Empathy is when you are so in tune with your own energy that you can sense the feelings and energy of others without a single word being spoken. It's the ability to give selflessly, offering your support or care without expecting anything in return.

When you have empathy, you no longer wish to see anyone in pain; instead, you strive to see everyone happy. This creates a cycle of energy that ultimately returns to you. It is another key to enlightenment, bringing you one step closer to your true self—being good, being at peace, and being one with all.

Forgiveness

Matthew 6:14

For if you forgive other people when they sin against you, your heavenly Father will also forgive you.

"If one does not forgive, what benefit have they brought to themselves or others? Forgiveness is a way of showing the other that there is light at the end of the tunnel."

To truly forgive others, you must first learn to forgive yourself. When you forgive yourself, healing begins from within, and you will find the light and peace that come with it. If someone wrongs you, pray for them.

Pray, "Thank you, God, for showing me the light, peace, courage, and love. I pray that they may see the light I see, feel the peace I feel, and gain the courage I have found. I pray they gain the wisdom and faith I have gained, and I hope they come to believe in the power of God, who created the universe for our souls, as I have come to believe. I pray for your healing, that you may become one with your soul, and that you too may recognise the light within."

When you pray from the heart, using your own words, you will come to realise that forgiveness is the true healer. You may not be able to control others, but you can have faith that they too will find healing in their own time. To help others, you must first see the light within yourself, for only then can you guide others to it.

Courage

Courage is the inner strength that resides within us, a power granted to us from the very beginning. It is the force embedded in our true essence, enabling us to face challenges and accomplish the purpose we were meant to fulfil on this earth.

With courage, there is no room for fear, for there is nothing beyond our reach. It is our truth, shining brightly within us. Have the courage to speak your truth, pursue what ignites your passion, and take bold action without fear. Do your best, trusting that everything will unfold as it is meant to, in perfect timing.

It is the key to our true power—the power of the universe, the power of light, the power of God.

Patience

Patience is a quality that either comes naturally or develops through experience. It is a virtue that fosters peace and builds trust, creating a sense of calm and understanding.

When we have patience, we have faith. When we have faith, we are one with God.

Embrace the profound connection with the universe and its beautiful, unspoken language.

"The universal language is the voice within you—the voice of your soul, the voice of the divine presence that resides within."

You might wonder, *How do I listen to this voice?*

This inner voice resides within every human being. Some naturally hear it with ease; others learn to tune into it over time, while some choose to dismiss its presence, unaware that we are more than just our physical selves.

Quieting the mind and stilling our thoughts is the doorway to this inner voice. Our restless minds and fleeting thoughts act as barriers, closing the door to this profound and intelligent power within.

A child can be born and grow up without ever feeling curious about the world or questioning the meaning behind all they see, touch, smell, and experience as humans. They absorb the knowledge offered to them, some excelling in it while others may not. Life continues, following the rhythm of millions before them—pursuing jobs, careers, families, or perhaps having none of these. Yet, regardless of the path, life inevitably moves forward.

Then there are those who, from childhood, possess a mind full of wonder. They question everything: Why is a cloud called a cloud? Who created the language we speak? Why is the sky blue? Why do we have two legs instead of four? Their curiosity is boundless, a never-ending journey of discovery. These individuals often grow up with a fascination for life that transcends the ordinary. If they are brave enough to follow this path, they will never stop learning, always seeking answers to their endless questions. Over time, their enquiries may extend beyond what the human mind can easily grasp, venturing into realms unseen—realms that are invisible to most but vivid and real to those who are awake and attuned to them.

Once you understand the language of the universe, the concept of being alone fades away. The word "alone" holds no meaning for someone who perceives beyond the surface of reality. Everything around us speaks, and everything carries a message—if only we open the senses that go beyond the limits of the mind and learn to truly see.

When we say we are never alone, it is because this deeper perception unites us with our higher self, which is in harmony with the entire universe. In this state of unity, every action, thought, and intention becomes visible in ways that transcend the physical. Here, one can never witness acts of unkindness, even if it's not from other people.

For example, if we tell a lie, the person being lied to may never know, but if we are connected to our soul, we feel the weight of it—because the universe knows. Similarly, if we commit an act of betrayal, even when it seems impossible for the other person to find out, the energy of that act reverberates. The universe sends messages, and their higher self often senses the truth. This interconnected awareness fosters a life of integrity, honesty, and kindness, as every action aligns with a greater cosmic accountability.

Then, there is a group of people who may not have been born curious but find their perspective shifting as life takes them through various changes. Over time, they begin to question their existence, the world around them, and the deeper meaning behind it all. These individuals may come to realise that the universe has a language—a profound and intricate communication beyond words—and that it holds layers unseen by the physical eyes. For those who learn to see beyond, hear beyond, and feel beyond the surface, we often refer to them as awakened.

Of course, learning our mother tongue is essential for basic communication. We rely on verbs, vowels, and structure to express ourselves and to navigate life. For those unable to speak, sign language offers a powerful alternative. These forms of language are vital to survival and connection in the physical world. Yet, beyond this necessity lies a universal language, one that transcends spoken words and is accessible to those who attune themselves to the deeper vibrations of existence.

But did you know there's another language—a universal language? This is a language spoken not with words but through a deep connection with our higher self, our soul. It is the language of energy, intuition, and interconnectedness. This profound communication encompasses everything in existence, including human telepathy.

If one learns this universal language, one unlocks limitless possibilities. It is a profound power gifted to us as humans—a means to seek, understand, and uncover true answers through this extraordinary form of communication.

You can communicate with the Universe, and the Universe can communicate with you. This is what we call signs. Signs are all around you; you just need to listen and observe. It's a unique language. Have you ever noticed angelic signs? Or how plants, birds, clouds, and so much more can offer you guidance? The world is speaking to you; it's a matter of tuning in to hear and see the messages.

It is all true, without a doubt.

But you might wonder, *How can I learn this language?*

The truth is you already know it. As a baby, you instinctively communicated through this language. It is your soul, which is deeply intelligent, that understands this language more profoundly than the words you speak.

The language we speak is of the ego—it is limited. Even though there are many languages in the world, their meanings remain essentially the same, which highlights a boundary. However, the language of the universe is limitless. It flows endlessly, and the more you open yourself to it, the more it unfolds.

Power of Prayers

"Instead of focusing on what you don't have, shift your attention to what you do have, for you already possess more than enough to be grateful for."

Prayers hold immense power over our well-being, both mentally and physically. A simple prayer can soothe the mind and alleviate physical pain. You may wonder, is this through magic? Not at all. There is no magic involved. What prayer truly does is awaken the soul, drawing out the inner light that has been waiting to rise.

Prayer can be a part of daily religious duty, but that is not what matters most. What truly matters is the sincerity behind every word you speak during prayer. It is not about where you pray, but how deeply connected you feel to the words you are saying and the intention behind them.

In prayer, it is first important to express gratitude to God and the universe for all they have provided to you, your surroundings, and all of humanity. Then, offer an apology for any wrongdoings you may have committed in the past, as well as for the harm others may have caused to any human being. Next, practise forgiveness for any actions that may have been done to you. Afterwards, share your heartfelt wishes for what you desire in life. Finally, pray for the happiness and well-being of yourself and every soul on this earth, wishing for health, peace, and joy for all.

Appreciation

When you begin to appreciate the things you have, you start to realise that there is an endless list of things to be thankful for. No matter who you are, where you are, or what your position in life may be, we all have countless blessings to appreciate. The list can begin with the simplest things: I am thankful to be alive, I am thankful for the opportunity to be on this earth, I am grateful to open my eyes and witness the morning light, I am thankful for the beauty of the sky, I am grateful to hear the songs of the birds, and I am thankful for the precious life I have been given.

Consider a scenario where a car hits a person, causing them to lose both of their legs. The next day, when they wake up in the hospital bed, they can still choose gratitude. They can be thankful for being alive, thankful that they only lost their legs, thankful for the lesson that the accident brings to their soul, and thankful for still being able to see the light of a new day. Similarly, if a person suddenly loses all their wealth, they can still find reasons to be grateful. They can be thankful for their health, thankful for the gift of life, and thankful that what they lost was only material wealth. No matter the situation, there is always something to be grateful for.

By practising gratitude, you will come to realise how fortunate you are to have what you do. You will begin to appreciate the things you may have previously overlooked or taken for granted. Through this practice, you are healing your soul, and as your inner light grows, it will radiate outward, touching and uplifting the beings around you.

Apology

When you apologise for your mistakes, you are acknowledging your actions and taking responsibility. By recognising these mistakes, you create an opportunity for self-healing and growth, allowing you to avoid repeating the same patterns in the future.

A mistake can be as simple as not smiling at your neighbour or as serious as causing harm to another being. Deep within your soul, you know when your actions have not aligned with your true essence.

Forgiveness

Extend forgiveness to all those who may have wronged you in your life. By forgiving them, you also forgive yourself, freeing your heart from resentment and suffering.

Forgive them, pray for them, and wish them happiness. May they find awakening and peace in their journey.

Wish

Wish for what you desire in life if it harms no one and helps you become a better version of yourself. Never doubt for a moment that your wish can come true. With faith and trust, anything is possible.

Pray for Everyone

Lastly, pray for all of humankind, wishing happiness, joy, wisdom, harmony, and peace for everyone. In doing so, you draw closer to the universe and recognise that we are all one, connected without separation.

Prayer is one of the most powerful forms of healing for our souls. You can practise it at any time and in any place. The most impactful moments to pray are at night, before sleep, and in the morning, as soon as you wake up. At night, your soul finds peace and rest, and in the morning, your ego can find peace to guide you through the day.

Power of Meditation

Meditation is another powerful way to connect with your soul and free yourself from the influence of your mind and ego. Through meditation, you can hear the voice of God within you – the inner voice, or intuition – that guides you toward clarity and truth.

Meditation is incredibly important because it offers a sacred time away from the outside world, a break from the noise of the material realm. It's a space where we can dream without limitations, free from the constraints of our ego or the voices of others telling us what's possible. In this peaceful state, we can soar like a bird, envisioning limitless possibilities and hearing the affirmation that all is achievable if we trust and believe. During meditation, we tap into the wisdom that guides us, revealing the steps we can take to manifest our deepest desires.

Through meditation and prayer, you journey to a higher realm, transcending both your body and mind. In this space, you become a radiant light, moving faster than any bird, effortlessly soaring through dimensions beyond the physical.

It is a time solely for yourself, a precious opportunity to embrace. In these moments, you become one with your soul, with God, and with the higher energies that surround you. This time should be cherished and invested wisely, with grace and intention.

Many believe that meditation must be done at specific times of the day or in certain positions. However, in my experience, meditation can be practised at any time and in any body position. What truly matters is learning to detach from your body and mind. Once you master this, you enter a meditative state, even while walking down the road.

There are no rules, no limitations. It is simply quieting the mind and allowing your soul to take over your entire being.

Power of Creative Visualisation

The power we all possess is incredible. We possess the ability to travel, see, feel, and experience through our imagination. Our souls can journey beyond boundaries, explore the unseen wonders of the universe, and feel things that the mind alone cannot comprehend.

If you can visualise your desires, know that with faith and courage, you have the power to manifest them in the physical world. However, always remember that your desires must serve the greater good—both for yourself and for others. If your intentions don't align with this, the universe might still bring your desires to you, but not for the reasons you anticipate. Instead, it may guide you through difficult lessons in ways you could never anticipate, teaching you valuable truths along the way.

Another benefit of visualisation is that when you find yourself in a situation, you'd rather escape but cannot physically leave, you can simply escape within. By using the power of your mind, you can create a mental sanctuary, allowing you to disconnect from the discomfort and find peace in your inner world.

For example, imagine you're stuck in an elevator and know you'll have to wait for the janitor to arrive in a few hours. There's no way out, and waiting is your only option. What do you do during these hours? You have a choice: you can panic, cry, or blame yourself for not leaving earlier, or you can resent the situation and complain that it's unfair. But what if you chose to enjoy your time in the elevator instead? How could you make the most of this time?

Simply by visualising a place you'd like to be in at that moment, you can escape the constraints of time and space. Imagine that there are no boundaries, no rules, just endless possibilities. You can envision yourself travelling to as many places as you wish, experiencing whatever you desire, and being with whoever you choose. In the world of visualisation, you are free—like a bird unburdened by anything. Interestingly, if someone is hungry and can't find food at that moment, they can visualise eating, and surprisingly, they may feel a sense of satisfaction in real life.

Creative visualisation is one of the most powerful tools we have as humans to create endless happiness within ourselves.

Power of Sound

Music and sound are powerful forms of connection to our souls. They resonate deeply, elevating the mind to higher vibrations and creating a sense of unity with our inner selves.

Have you ever experienced a headache that seemed to disappear after listening to music? Or felt lost, only to find clarity and solutions through the power of sound? Perhaps you've struggled to concentrate while studying, but after listening to music, you suddenly found yourself able to focus for hours.

Yes, music and sound have a profound impact on our state of mind. While everyone has their taste in music, the most healing sounds are often those without lyrics. Lyrics belong to the realm of the mind, which tends to focus on the meaning of words and stir thoughts. On the other hand, instrumental music, or music without lyrics, can reach the soul directly, allowing the mind to release its need for meaning and creating space for deeper, more peaceful resonance.

When you listen to sounds that resonate with your soul, you become attuned to every subtle detail. It's as if you enter another dimension—one without boundaries or limitations. You'll feel like a bird soaring freely in any direction it chooses. Sounds that connect with your soul have the power to liberate your mind, freeing you from the constraints of ego and allowing you to experience pure freedom.

Memories

I would like to share some of my personal experiences with connecting to the universe and communicating with it.

Before we dive into this chapter, I want to emphasise that I firmly believe that each of us can connect with the universe. Some may have more advanced abilities, but this is often the result of personal growth through suffering, life experiences, or simply by quieting the mind. We are all souls, and at our core, we are all one. The sense of division we experience on this earth is an illusion created by our egos. Ultimately, there is no separation when we return home to the universe.

I receive messages through dreams, visions, voices, numbers, animals, clouds, feathers, coins—essentially, through everything and anything around me. This ability comes from learning to quiet my mind, allowing me to connect with higher energies and be receptive to the signs and guidance the universe provides.

1.

It was my final year of undergraduate studies, and my capstone project involved composing a piece of music for a small chamber orchestra. I chose a poem that featured eight historical characters. Interestingly, an art museum in Dublin was showcasing an exhibition inspired by this very poem, marking the source of the poet's inspiration.

At that time, I was living in Glasgow, and there was a fire within me—one that I later recognised as the voice of my soul urging me to visit the gallery. Without hesitation, I booked a flight for the next day, planning to fly in the morning and return in the evening. Once I arrived, I visited the gallery and requested to see the original photographs related to the poem for my project. We were taken to the basement, where I had the opportunity to view them closely and take a few snapshots to use as reference while composing.

I spent a few hours in the gallery during my time in Dublin, and without realising it, I quieted my mind and began to absorb the energy of the poet and the characters. By the time I left, I felt a deep sense of joy, knowing that visiting the gallery had been the right choice, as I had connected with the energy there. Upon returning to Glasgow, I placed all eight-character images in front of me and began composing a theme for each. At that moment, I truly felt that the pictures came alive—each one seemed to communicate the specific instrument it wanted, guiding my composition.

I thought I was losing my mind. A few days later, it was time to meet with my tutor. I shared my experience with him—about my trip, my visit to the gallery, and how each picture seemed to send me a message about which instrument to use.

I nervously asked, "I must be going crazy, right?"

He looked at me and said, "Not at all. You've just become a composer, an artist."

2.

I have a vivid memory from my 20s when I decided to take some time off to focus on writing music. With plenty of quiet moments on my hands, I would spend hours each afternoon walking in the park, watching the sunset as I reflected and let my thoughts flow.

During my walks, I began to experience things that I couldn't understand at the time, as I didn't yet trust in my ability to perceive beyond the ordinary. I often saw large, towering figures in white, standing on either side of the path I always walked. They would bow and offer me flowers.

When I returned home, I couldn't help but think, *I must have truly lost my mind.*

A few months later, I completed the music I had been working on. For some light entertainment, I went with a friend to see a spiritual reader. This is where things took a surprising turn.

She looked at me and said, "I see angels bowing and offering you flowers as a thank you for writing music through their voices."

I was in complete disbelief. She was describing exactly what I had experienced just a few weeks earlier. Despite this, I struggled to trust my abilities once again.

3.

This memory may not be the most pleasant, but it holds valuable insight into the power of dreams. For two months, I kept having the same recurring dream.

In the dream, my mother and sister were in the car—my sister driving and my mother seated beside her. They approached a roundabout, and suddenly, a bus collided with their car. The accident was severe. The dream then shifted, taking me to another vision where I saw my sister, but my mother was no longer there.

For two months, I kept having the same recurring dream, and I would constantly warn my family to be cautious while driving. Then, one night, around midnight, I was asleep when the phone rang a few times, waking me up. The name on the screen was my sister's. I answered, but the voice on the other end wasn't my sister's—it was our neighbour, who lived next door.

She told me, "Your sister's had an accident. A van hit her badly, and she's unconscious in the hospital."

My heart sank.

I asked, "Is she alive?"

The neighbour replied, "Yes, but she might lose her legs."

Fortunately, my sister's legs survived, albeit with severe damage. As she prepared to return home from the hospital three months later, we received devastating news—our mother's diagnosis with stage four cancer. Eight months later, she passed away. Reflecting on the repeated dreams I had during those two months, I now see they were a warning, a kind of heads-up for what was to come. Certain aspects of life are beyond our control, unchangeable due to their predetermined course.

4.

My mother spent her final month in hospice. None of us knew when her time would come to leave us.

Her feet were swollen, painful, and turned a bluish colour. We reached out to her every day, but the pain persisted. We decided it might be more helpful to bring in a professional who specialises in reflexology to provide some relief.

We began searching and were fortunate to find someone who could come as soon as possible, not knowing how much time my mother had left. One afternoon, we were able to arrange for the lady to come the following morning at 9 a.m.

We were relieved to have found someone so quickly, ensuring that my mother could benefit from the experience. As the night approached, I went to bed early, knowing I needed to drive to the hospice in the morning. That night, I had a dream.

In the dream, I entered the hospice, and it was eerily quiet and empty.

Then, I noticed a metal door slowly opening, revealing an overwhelming light. As I stepped closer, I saw that the light seemed to stretch into an endless tunnel, glowing with a brilliance that seemed to go on forever.

When I was a child, I remember my mother telling me stories about a tunnel of light. She was always fascinated by the afterlife and the universe, having had her own experiences of seeing things in dreams. She often told me that when a person leaves their body, they enter this tunnel of light, a journey that takes them into the unknown.

When I woke up from the dream, I instinctively knew that she had passed. As I reached for my phone, I saw a message from my sister, sent just an hour before I had woken up. In her text, she wrote, "Mom is gone. She left us a few hours ago."

5.

I don't recall exactly how many nights passed after my mother was gone, but every night, I had vivid dreams of travelling alongside her through her journey.

Every night, I was with her, and each night she found herself in a different place. The first place resembled her room in the hospice, but it wasn't quite the same—it was more like a reflection of it. She lay on her bed, still unwell.

On the second night, she appeared in a vast, empty, dark space. This time, she was standing, and there was no trace of illness.

On the third night, the space seemed brighter, and she was trying on sparkling clothes.

She turned to me and said, "You need to see a doctor," then pointed at my stomach.

Naturally, I ignored it.

On the fourth night, she was in a garden, appearing as if she were a force of nature, deeply connected to the earth.

Each night after that, she moved to a larger, greener space. The last dream I had of her during those nights was in a stunning, vibrant place. She sat on a large golden chair, wearing a flowing yellow dress. She looked healthy and happy, radiating joy. The surroundings were breathtakingly beautiful.

The *Divine Comedy* by Dante is one of the works I came to know many years after all of this. Its depiction closely mirrors what I saw in the dream. It explains that there is life after death and that, as souls, we must pass through various levels to reach the light.

Three months later, one night I experienced excruciating pain that sent me to the emergency room. The doctors initially suspected appendicitis, so they performed surgery that same night. However, the doctors diagnosed me with ovarian cancer, removed it, and everything is now fine.

My mother sent me a warning through a dream.

6.

There was a time when I felt utterly alone, and the only things that kept me going were hope, prayers, and my trust in the universe.

During this time, I underwent a profound transformation. I felt an overwhelming closeness to my soul, to God, to the universe, to angels, and all the unseen forces around me.

During this time, I received countless messages that made me feel as though I was losing my mind. Although I had experienced similar instances in the past, where things later came to pass, this time it felt overwhelming. I was receiving messages through dreams while I slept and, during the day, in the form of visions, numbers, music, birds, animals, feathers, and coins. Everything seemed so surreal.

It wasn't until I started reading books by chance that I discovered others had similar experiences. That's when everything I had seen and felt began to make sense. One night, as I was reading, I had a dream in which I found a massive book, among other things. When I woke up, I dismissed it, but a week later, I felt an unexpected urge to write down all my experiences, as well as the things I had witnessed throughout my life that had shaped me. After a few days of writing, I remembered the dream about the book, and it suddenly clicked—it was part of the bigger plan.

Miracle

Miracles are the power within us, accessible if we choose to believe in them. To put it simply, one will experience a miracle if they truly believe it is possible but will not receive one if they only believe it might happen.

To be alive is a miracle. Each of us is a miracle, created to bring joy to the world. We all carry a unique, invisible light around our physical form—some can see it, while others cannot.

Law of Attraction

"You are the spirit of God, and He has bestowed upon you the light to shine. You have the power to manifest anything you desire, as long as you pour all your energy and joy into His creation on this earth."

Fear begets fear, love begets love, happiness begets happiness, and sadness begets sadness. Which one do you choose? The power is yours and yours alone. Find your purpose, find peace, and discover your heaven.

Quiet your mind. All the answers you seek are already within you. Happiness and joy reside within you. Light and peace are within you. The beauty of life is within you. All you need to do is nothing—simply cease thinking.

Remember, miracles happen all the time. However, to access them, one must truly believe in them from the deepest part of their being. Have you ever wondered why children are so drawn to cartoons that feature magical miracles? Children, with their pure hearts and without the influence of ego, naturally believe that anything is possible—that miracles can bring about anything. As adults, we may lose this beautiful quality as our egos block our ability to believe in the unexpected gifts the universe has to offer.

Your purpose as a human on this earth is not to lose this quality but to nurture it and allow it to flourish throughout your life. You achieve this by believing, accepting, and trusting in the purpose of everything, which guides you to uncover your inner light. It is through this journey that you will recognise that the doorway to heaven exists within you; by letting go of the emotional burdens you've created throughout your life by listening to your ego. By believing in the energy that surpasses our known reality, we can manifest heaven. The timeless Disney film *Cinderella* provides one of the greatest examples. What an incredible, truly inspiring story—it offers a powerful lesson to all of humankind.

The lesson in this story is clear and powerful. It teaches us about human kindness, hope, inner happiness, and the unseen energies the universe offers when we believe. It also highlights the consequences of being unkind, manipulative, deceitful, and dishonest. The story shows that while the path to success may seem easier when fuelled by negative traits, such actions will ultimately bring harm in the most unexpected ways. This is the law of attraction—what you give is what you receive. Cinderella, no matter her circumstances—whether as a servant mistreated or a princess honoured—created her heaven by choosing happiness. On the other hand, her stepmother, driven by greed, jealousy, and manipulation, created her hell, along with the suffering of her daughters.

This story also touches on the unexplainable communication between the character and her surroundings. While it is magical, it can be difficult to believe that such communication could exist in human life. However, it hints at the idea that the universe has its language. This doesn't mean that objects like forks will speak to you, but rather that, if you quiet your mind, you can receive signs from everything around you. Despite lacking scientific proof, some awakened individuals may experience this in their lives.

As humans, we often say, "We need a job to survive. You're saying our main purpose is to awaken, but surely that doesn't address the practical aspects of daily life." The answer is this: Yes, your primary purpose is to awaken. Once you awaken, you will comprehend your true human purpose in life. If your job or career is aligned with your true purpose, it will ignite your inner light and resonate with your authentic self. From there, you will naturally shine. When your work is truly your calling, it becomes an endless source of energy, allowing you to give your best without effort. It won't even feel like a job because you will be fulfilled with the light and love from your soul.

From there, success and abundance will flow into your life.

The universe, a source of infinite beauty, connects everything we do on this earth to its energy source. To tap into this energy, you must connect with your soul, as it is the mechanism that links you to this divine power. The ego, on the other hand, is a mechanism that remains grounded at the earthly level, which is limited.

Remember, when you ask the universe for what you truly desire, it can and will manifest—especially if your intentions are for the greater good of yourself and others. With patience and trust, there is nothing beyond your reach.

However, it is crucial to remember that once you ask, you should not continue to dwell on it. You can pray or meditate on it, but avoid overthinking. Constantly thinking about it creates doubt, which blocks the flow of energy. The mind, with its doubts, can hinder the energy that the universe is trying to bring to you.

Trust that it will happen in due time, and it will. There is no need to overthink it.

True Love

You are my everything. You are my life. You are my twin soul. You are my heaven. You are my joy. You are my love. You are my family. You are my other half. You are my spiritual partner. You are the miracle of this earth. You are perfection. You are beautiful, inside and out. You are the light that shines upon this world. You are my star.

We have united to accomplish incredible things on this earth, serving humanity—this is our purpose. As one, we stand strong, each bringing qualities the other may lack, completing each other's soul. I have unwavering faith and absolute trust in the universe that you and I will fulfil our mission, united.

God, the angels, and the universe have all sent me signs that you are. I have complete faith in their truth. My happiness lies in seeing you happy.

My joy comes from witnessing your smile. My love is unconditional. My wish is not one of attachment but a genuine desire—to be a part of your happiness, united. My words come from my higher self, free from the ego that might hinder my true feelings. They are God's words, flowing through me to touch your beautiful soul. Remember, I love you for who you truly are—your higher self. Miracles happen all the time; true love exists.

True love is a concept that many often misunderstand. It is not just a feeling but a deep connection between us as humans and everything around us. When you give fully to the universe and its people, you begin to see that life is truly beautiful. In this chapter, we will explore the nature of true love between two individuals—partners. While the unconditional love between a mother and child is undeniably profound, we will focus on the unique bond shared between two people who choose to walk through life together.

What exactly is unconditional love? Unconditional love is the essence of true love. It is the deep affection you feel for someone, not based on their actions or appearance, but for who they truly are at the core. It is love for their soul, transcending their ego. The ego, after all, changes over time, making it an unreliable foundation for love. Unconditional love remains constant, rooted in acceptance and understanding beyond the surface.

When such a connection exists, it forms the most beautiful union. It's important to understand that these unions are not by chance—they happen because both individuals share a soul mission that can only be fulfilled together. This mission is to help others awaken and realise their potential, bringing light and transformation to the world.

People often refer to this as the 'twin flame' concept. It is as if you are experiencing yourself in another body. You come into this world with shared experiences—past, and present, and a common vision for the future. The connection is divinely supported, deeply telepathic, and feels surreal in its depth.

This bond is unlike any other. It emerges when least expected, a connection that is divinely orchestrated by God's plan. It often manifests between older, more enlightened souls, those who carry light within. When these two come together, they hold a magical light that has the power to heal and elevate the earth, drawing it closer to the realms of heaven.

In the end, love is the highest form of energy and vibration. Love has the power to heal us all and draw us closer to heaven. Our true purpose on this earth is to love and to share that love with others.